Volume 1 Number 2   Summer 1978

PAPERBACK QUARTERLY

"A JOURNAL FOR PAPERBACK COLLECTORS"

CONTENTS

The Pecan Valley Press
Brownwood, Texas

The Paperback Quarterly will feature articles and notes dealing with every type (mystery, science fiction, detective, western, adventure, etc.) and with every aspect of new, old, and rare paperbacks. Emphasis will be placed on the historical research of paperbacks, their authors, illustrators, publishers, and distributors; but the editors also invite contributions of bibliographical interest. In short, the only criterion for the editor's consideration is that the subject matter pertain only to paperbacks. In addition to articles and notes, the PQ will feature a section for the review of both old and new paperback originals.

The PQ will be published in March, June, September, and December of each year with a subscription rate of $4.00 per year or individual copies at $1.25 each. Institutional and library subscriptions are $6.00 per year

All correspondence, articles, notes, queries, book reviews or books for review and subscriptions should be sent to: 1710 Vincent, Brownwood, Texas 76801

Billy C. Lee...............Co-Editor
Charlotte Laughlin.........Co-Editor
Bill Crider...............Contributing Editor
Tessica Martin............Photographer
Cover Printer.............Martin E. Gottschalk

LETTERS

Dear Sir:

I just received the first issue of the Paperback Quarterly. As I am primarily interested in collecting 1940's paperbacks, I particularly enjoyed the articles on paperback originals and Harry Whittington. Robert E. Howard & L. Sprague de Camp are covered well enough in the Science Fiction and Fantasy publications, without having half of this issue devoted to them. Also, (see bottom of page 23,) the Karl Edward Wagner Kane books are not a continuation of Howard's Solomon Kane stories.

Regarding Paperback Originals, could you get Mr Crider to go into more detail about why the hardcover publishers were so opposed to the paperback originals? This was not at all clear from his article. I know that hardcover publishers got a share of the paperback royalties and would have resented having Gold Medal get a book that they wanted. However, at that time, I would think that nearly all authors would have sold to a hardcover publisher over a paperback company it they could find a hardback firm that would buy the book. I thought it was only in the last 10-15 years that paperback firms have been able to outbid hardcover firms.

From Notes & Queries #4, Novel Library books were published by Diversey Publications which was either a subsidiary of Avon or was originally an independent firm which was then acquired by Avon. By 1948, Diversey's office was at the same address as Avon, and each company regularly advertised the others books. The difference in price you mention probably is due to there being digest editons of Untamed Darling and Rites of Love. Although I cannot be sure that these titles were published as 35¢ digests, many Avon & Diversey books were issued in both formats with the different prices. Since the ad you mention was from #384, the editions of Woodford's books would have been #409 & #403. Since these would have been planned editions, Avon may have intended to raise their prices to 35¢, but then changed their mind & issued both books

at 25¢. With books in the early 400's, Avon did
begin raising prices on some titles to 35¢.
  Yours truly,
  Dave Killian
  Tacoma, Washington

Dear Billy Lee:
  Although it has taken me quite a while to get
around to reading the first issue of PAPERBACK QUARTERLY
I finally did so--and with considerable enjoyment.
  I applaud in particular the information and inter-
views on paperback authors. Perhaps as PQ progresses
and ultimately pays its own way you will be able to
publish similar material about paperback cover artists.
I am a Bob McGinnis fan of long standing, and admire
the work of other cover artists as well. In the best
of all possible worlds, may you prosper to the point
where more and better illustrations will become part
of your publication.
  You have made a commendable start. We live in
the midst of an era of such popularity of the paperback
form of book that we may tend to overlook its riches.
PQ is in the vanguard of what may some day be a bonanza
of publications devoted to this vast arm of popular
publishing. Can you imagine what it would have been
like if someone had started a similar quarterly devoted
to the pulp magazines when they were in their prime?
PQ stands on that threshold in the world of paperbacks.
And who is to say paperbacks will not someday follow
the pulps into limbo? No one foresaw that fate for
the pulps, but it happened. And who dares say paperbacks are immune?
  I do hope you will be a leader in the struggle
to obtain more recognition for the cover artists
whose work has so much to do with successful rack sales
of paperbacks. They go largely unheralded and un-
acknowledged. I'd like to see a drive started to push
the publishers into crediting the cover artist. Too
often not only is there no credit line, but also the
artist's name is cropped from the final printed version,

or never was there in the first place.
Good fortune in your venture.
Cordially,
Al Fick
Amsterdam, New York

[Editor's Note: We agree Al; Not enough credit is given to paperback cover artists. We welcome any article about or interview with a paperback cover artist.]

Dear Editors:
Having read Paperback Quarterly vol 1, no. 1 from cover to cover, I can say it is first rate. I found it to be most enjoyable, especially the article on Robert E. Howard's Library. I have always been interested in the books people keep around them and whose library could possible be more interesting than the library of Robert E. Howard?
I have often wondered where Howard got the name of Conan for his most famous character. I have always assumed that it did come from the name of Arthur Conan Doyle. Mostly, I guess, because until recently, Doyle's name was the only other instance in which I had ever encountered the rare name. But now, I think your readers might like to know of another reference to a Conan, Duke Conan IV, whose daughter married the son of Henry II of England. This account can be found on page 17 of the book Rambles in Brittany by Francis Miltown, The Page Co., Boston 2nd ed., 1918.
I am looking forward to the listing of more books belonging to R.E.H. and also more good reading and information about paperbacks.
Sincerely,
Robert M. Williams
Rule, Texas

a dragline.

One of Faulkner's most inspired creations, however, is a roadhouse with a perfect name: Little Chicago. What visions of depravity that name could conjure up in a southern hill man! It could probably give the visions a touch of reality, too, at least as it's described in Cabin Road:

> The ceiling was pocked with holes. In several places the rear ends of the lead bullets were sticking out of the rough boarding, as if the guns that had fired them had not been powerful enough to drive them from sight. There were some of these bullets embedded in the walls at shoulder height (p. 79).

The boards in which these bullets (from Derringers and Owlheads, Ex-Senator explains) are stuck and "nailed only at the top, loosely, and could be flipped out from the bottom in full stride if anyone wished quick exit from Little Chicago" (p. 77).

The government is another source of humor. Almost all of Cabin Road revolves around a government man's attempt to present Jones Peabody with a check; but Jones can't sign his name, and no one else can sign as witness to his mark because no one else in the neighborhood can write, either. No one could cash the check even if Jones could sign for it. The government man wanders from Uncle Good's place to Little Chicago trying to get change for a five dollar bill. No one has it. Ain't Gonna Rain No More introduces Miss Green, a welfare worker who has as little success as the government man when because of the drought Cabin Road is declared a disaster area: all the money allocated to the county is spent on the special manufacture of one 75 X 5-½ rubber tire which can be inflated to 115 pounds of pressure for George Shaw's 1917 Packard.

It's a shame that the paperback novels of John Faulkner didn't get the critical attention they deserved in the 1950s. Their paperback format was no

doubt part of the problem. I believe that they are
classic examples of a fast-disappearing form of
American humor, minor classics, maybe, but classics
nevertheless. They're well worth searching for, and
if you find one, read it. If you find <u>Uncle Good's
Girls</u>, send it to me.

Can You Match These
Characters To Their Authors?

a. Inspector McKee	1. John Evans
b. The Saint	2. Frank Gruber
c. Topper	3. Kelley Roos
d. Johnny Fletcher	4. Helen Reilly
e. Conan	5. Leslie Ford
f. Colonel Primrose	6. Dashiell Hammett
g. Sheriff Henry Conroy	7. Leslie Charteris
h. Paul Pine	8. Maxwell Grant
i. The Shadow	9. Thorne Smith
j. Jeff Troy	10. George Harmon Coxe
k. Nick Charles	11. W.C. Tuttle
l. Michael Shayne	12. Robert E. Howard
m. Kent Murdock	13. Erle Stanley Gardner
n. Perry Mason	14. Brett Halliday

(answers on page 47)

This book is of the earth, and so
are its ribald, hilarious people

CABIN ROAD

JOHN FAULKNER

14

ELMER KELTON

Elmer Kelton was born in Andrews County, Texas, the son of a cowboy. Though he has been a free-lance writer most of his career, he has been in his words, "a newspaperman first." He was the farm and ranch editor of the San Angelo Standard-Times for 15 years from 1948-1963. In 1963 he became editor of the Ranch magazine until 1968 when he assumed the position of associate editor of the West Texas Livestock Weekly.

His entire life has been centered around farm and ranch life, cowboys and cattle. This experience has proven itself in his many award winning western novels. He has won the Western Writers of America Spur Award three times: Buffalo Wagons (1957), The Day the Cowboys Quit (1972), and The Time It Never Rained (1974). In 1974 he won the National Cowboy Hall of Fame Western Heritage Award for The Time It Never Rained. In 1977, two of his westerns were selected,(The Day The Cowboys Quit and The Time It Never Rained),for the "25 Best Westerns Of All Time As Selected By Western Writers Of American" list.

It's hard for most people to categorize Kelton's writings. They're not exactly what you classify as the typical shoot'em up western. Though fiction, they're historically sound with down to earth realism thats unique to Kelton.

His many books include:
Ballantine Books: (Paperback Originals)

Hot Iron, 1955
Buffalo Wagons, 1956
Barbed Wire, 1957
Shadow Of A Star, 1959
The Texas Rifles, 1960
Donovan, 1961
Bitter Trail, 1962
Horsehead Crossing, 1963

Massacre At Goliad, 1965
Llano River, 1966
After the Bugles, 1967
Captain's Rangers, 1968
Hanging Judge, 1969
Bowie's Mine, 1971
Wagontongue, 1972

Paperback Library: (Paperback Original)
      Shotgun Settlement, 1969, under the house
           name, Alex Hawk

Doubleday:
      The Day The Cowboys Quit, 1971 (Paperback: Ace Books
      The Time It Never Rained, 1973 (Paperback: Ace Books
      The Good Old Boys, 1978
      Joe Pepper, 1975 under the pseudonym,
           Lee McElroy
      Lone Way To Texas, 1976 under the pseudonym,
           Lee McElroy

Talley Press, San Angelo:
      Looking Back West, 1972 a non-fiction
           compilation of articles

A PQ Interview With:

ELMER KELTON

PQ: Mr. Kelton, how many paperback originals have you written?

EK: Seventeen, sixteen of them published by Ballantine. I'll have to qualify that a little bit; the first two of them were bought out by Ballantine in paperback and hardcover simultaneously. You probably know that Ballantine experimented a little bit in the early years with simultaneous publication in hard and soft backs. In the first couple of years they operated they tried to publish all their books in both formats. They could sell the hardcovers to libraries, military service libraries, and so forth. And then the softcovers were for general trade. They went on with this dual format for awhile, but it evidently didn't turn out over the long run, and they just finally dropped it.

My third Ballantine book and all the following ones were brought out in soft covers only. The one paperback that I did that was not published by Ballantine was done under a straight sale contract with Paperback Library, and they used a house name, Alex Hawk. They tried a western series using their own house name and contracted with a number of western writers to do the books. There were eight or ten of those. The series only lasted a year or two. It wasn't successful because every writer just wrote his own story, and there was no continuation of characters or continuity of style. House names used to be fairly common in the early days, especially in magazines, the pulp magazine days.

PQ: Have you written under some pseudonyms of your own, aside from the house name Alex Hawk?

EK: I've had two Doubleday Westerns under the pseudonym Lee McElroy. Those books are *Joe Pepper* and *A Long Way to Texas*. They were both hardbacks, and *A Long Way to Texas* hasn't yet come out in paperback; but I expect Doubleday will sell the rights to it as they did to the first book.

I took the name Lee McElroy from two ranches where I spent time as a boy. My dad was on the McElroy Ranch in Chrane for 36 years and for some years he leased a place and had his own cattle on a place called the Lee Ranch. So when Doubleday wanted to put a pseudonym on my straight westerns as opposed to my bigger ones, I used those two ranch names.

PQ: Why did Doubleday want to put another name on these two westerns? [*Joe Pepper* and *A Long Way to Texas*]?

EK: *Straight westerns went into their western category called Double D Books and they're considered not as prestigious as their trade books. Since they already had two trade books from me under my own name, they didn't want to use my name on what they considered a little lesser category; then come back again and put my name on another trade book and maybe have it hampered.*

PQ: Who decides what category (straight or trade) westerns fit into?

EK: *I think they almost automatically categorize themselves. Traditional[straight] westerns will be shorter(50 to 60 thousand words) where as a book like The Good Old Boys[a trade book] is closer to 90 thousand words. The Good Old Boys would not fit into Double D, nobody gets killed, nobody even gets seriously powder burned, so it would not really fit into the straight western category. Neither one of them[Joe Pepper and A Long Way to Texas] was exactly conventional yet they had to*

19

fit there because they were basically action stories.

PQ: Is there any talk about making any of your books, say one of the Spur winners, into a movie?

EK: Talk, yes. But no action! I use a New York agent for my books, and he farms these things out to a Hollywood agent. They send what they consider my better books around, but nothing has come of it. There just aren't that many western movies being made any more. The Hollywood agents sent me two letters that came back from different studios concerning The Day the Cowboys Quit. One of them said that they sort of liked the general tone of the book, but they thought the plot was a little bit thin. The other one also liked the general tone of the book, but they thought the plot was too complicated! I had one group to go so far as to write a screen play of The Time It Never Rained, and a group of young fellows have written the complete screen play of Joe Pepper; but they're still trying to sell it. The way Hollywood works these days, most of these pictures are made by independents who have to raise their own money, and they distribute it through a major motion picture company. So these people have to finance the picture, and the money is hard to get.

PQ: What about television?

EK: I sold a few, I think three back in my pulp days; way back. Warner Brothers bought them all; I never saw any of them. They were pulp magazine stories. I imagine they bought them for a plot twist then they just adapted them to their characters; one was on Colt Forty-five, one on Maverick, and I forget what the other one was. I never did get to see any of them.

PQ: Into how many languages have your books been translated?

EK: I don't know exactly, but several. I've had pretty good luck with them in the Scandinavian countries, Norway, Sweden, several in German, one or two in Dutch and Spanish. The Spainsh translations that I've had have been sold in Spain; I don't know about Mexico and the South American countries. I've had a little criticism on my books for the European market that they're really not quite bloody enough. The main criticism that I've had is that they generally like their books full of action and somewhat bloody, and mine are not normally that way. They usually don't go into what you would call excessive violence. I'd rather write people stories. I think that's been a handicap that has kept me from selling anywhere in the league of say Louie L'Amour. He's a good writer, but he's a little more action-oriented than I am.

PQ: We've noticed that at many paperback displays, half the rack seems to be filled with Louis L'Amour books.

EK: Yes, that makes it pretty hard for other western writers to get a whole lot of display space. Bantam books is very alert and very agressive and they'll usually see to it that Louie L'Amour gets about half of the display space for westerns. Louie of course probably gets more sells that all the rest of us in the field put together. Thats may guess. His best book in my opion was Hondo published by Gold Medal. He writes a good story; its got a lot of movement, a lot of color and then of course he's well promoted. It's a combination of all these things.

PQ: Do you have any regrets that Ballentine didn't get out and agressively promote your books like Bantam did Louis L'Amour's?

EK: I always wished they had had the agressive sells techniques but I imagine you would have to say they didn't have the resources that Bantam had.

Ballantine was basically a small, family operation and didn't have their own distribution system. They always had to work through a distributor and I know a time or two they had a very traumatic experience when they changed distributors. I remember one or two of my books came out just at the time they made a change and the books all wound up stored in a warehouse somewhere and never did get out. Basically, this is one of the troubles with the paperback; they[distributors] kind of handle it by the pound and they really don't pay that much to individual titles. They work on a computor type system, selling in volume and you just get in there way when you try to deal in individual titles.

PQ: You began publishing paperback westerns a little over twenty years ago. How do you compare the market then and now? Was the market for paperback westerns better then?

EK: The market was better just before I got into it! My timing with my books has often been similar to my friends timing in livestock trading---It's always "You should have been here last week!" I had been writing pulp magazine stories--I sold my first one in 1947--and I had been doing pulp magazine stories for several years, particularly to Ranch Romances. My mother read Ranch Romances; that's how I came to grow up on them. When the pulps began to die out in the early 50's, my agent was after me to try a book. He said that the market for westerns in the future was going to be in paperbacks. I finally got up my nerve to tackle a book; I started it in 1952 or 1953. At this time the market was really good; all the paperback houses were booming. Ballantine was paying established authors $5,000 to $6,000 advances on paperback books, which in those days was big money. When I got mine finished and submitted the bottom had fallen out, and nobody even wanted to hear the word "western" spoken, much less read the manuscript. And my book bumped around for a year and a half before Ballantine picked it up. After that, I never had any trouble selling to Ballantine whatever I wrote.

PQ: You mentioned having an agent when you were still writing short stories for the pulps. How did you decide upon an agent?

EK: After I sold several stories on my own, I had letters from various agents wanting to take me on as a client; and this man had more western writers than the others so I decided on him.

PQ: Why did you decide to write in the western genre instead of some other field?

EK: Personal experience and personal preference. I always loved westerns. I grew up on a ranch around cowpunchers and heard all those old stories from all these old-timers as far back as I'm able to remember, and that is just my natural element.

I get a lot of comliments on my dialogue, but I just tell people that I write it like I talk it. I got that from my dad and my grandad and all those I grew up around, so I just mainly quote myself. My dad was a cowpuncher on the Scarborough Ranch in Andrews County[Texas]. I was born on that ranch.

PQ: What made you want to write anyway? You say that your background is in ranching, but there aren't very many ranchers who are also writers.

EK: Well, I wasn't a very good cowboy for one thing. In fact, I was a very poor cowboy. Any of the old-timers in Crane or Andrews County[Texas] can testify that I was probably the poorest cowboy that either one of those counties every produced. And I always loved to read from the time I learned how and I kind of wanted to write about as far back as I remember. I was a voracious reader as a boy. Anything in English I read.

PQ: What about the Spanish in your books? Do you read Spanish well, or do you have someone check the Spanish?

EK: I have someone check it. I took Spanish two years in school, and I came out of it probably poorer than I went in. I try to put in just enough Spanish flavor and still not confuse the reader, because I have to assume that my readers to not read Spanish so I have to make my meaning clear. I have a couple of friends of Mexican extraction who help me check the Spanish, and I had a friend in Crane who taught Spanish go over The Time It Never Rained. I also had it checked by a man around Kerrville who is interested in linguistics. He wrote a book on farm and ranch Spanish.

PQ: Mr. Kelton, who do you think is one of the best craftsmen in writing westerns?

EK: In the pure traditional western field I would have to go with Luke Short. He's been dead two or three years now, but his works are still current, and they may still have one or two of his unpublished yet. For pure craftsmanship of the traditional action western, I would have to choose Luke Short.

A.B. Guthrie, Ernest Haycox, and Eugene Manlove Rhodes are more "literary" writers. They're very good, but I don't rank them as simply traditional western writers. The early Ernest Haycox is traditional western, but his later works are more "literary."

PQ: What writers did you use as patterns for your writing?

EK: For awhile, all of them! I studied all of them pretty thoroughly. When you start out that way you need to. I studied Luke Short in particular and several others. But particularly him, because to me he was the epitome of the action-type western writer. Then after that I quit pattering him and just became myself, because the world only needed one Luke Short and only one Louie L'Amour. If you just copy these other fellows you're not really yourself; you're just a poor carbon copy of someone else. But you have to start somewhere.

PQ: What are some of your personal experiences with paperback publishing? Are paperback writers fairly paid?

EK: I don't know how to answer that--whether one is fairly paid. When I started into it, for the amount of work in doing the stories it was much better paying than the pulp magazines had been. On the other hand, I find that the pay scale for paperbacks, the category of western paperbacks, hasn't changed a whole lot in right at twenty years I've been in it. The purchasing power of the dollar has really dropped, yet out of the last paperback I did, I didn't earn a whole lot more than I did on the first one I did.

PQ: What about artistic freedom? Do you have publishers asking you to add a little bit of blood in order to get published or to get more money?

EK: No, most of my works were published by Ballantine, and they were very liberal with the writer's freedom. Ballantine didn't emphasize blood when they were publishing westerns, but they haven't published westerns in two or three years. Ian Ballantine and his wife sold out their interest in the company several years ago. It still carries their name, but it belongs to a conglomerate. When the Ballantines did it, they were very personal. Mrs. Ballantine, Betty Ballantine, was the editor, and she read all the manuscripts. It was her decision whether they bought or not. It was basically a family operation.

PQ: What are some advantages and disadvantages in publishing in paperback compared to those in publishing in hardback?

EK: *In my personal experience, I've gotten more money for hardbacks; but not all writers do. It depends on the situation. The advantages of paperback publishing are that usually you retain all publication rights other than first publication rights. Most of the time hardback publishers keep 50% of any subsidiary sales. Doubleday does not keep movie rights; if I were to sell one, it would be 100% mine; not all the publishers are like that. But I'm not holding my breath for one of my books to be made into a movie. I used to, but I've given that up.*

PQ: What do you think is the future of the western paperback?

EK: *I would imagine there has probably been a decline in overall unit sale over the years because younger people by enlarge don't appear to be picking up westerns as much; so probably the ones of us who are writing westerns maybe catoring to an older group thats increasingly getting older.*

Usually the popularity or sells in westerns has been in inverse relation to the number of westerns on television. When the television was just saturated with westerns, westerns in print form declined in sales. There's a market there of some form or another; when a die hard western fan can't get them on television then he reads them.

Westerns have always been with us, they have had their ups and downs. I don't think we'll see the end of the western in the forseeable future. Western paperbacks have a tendency to sell at a more of less predetermined rate. They can almost estimate how many copies will sell before they're printed. There is a market out there and it won't hardly slip up.

PQ: In your experience have you found paperback writing to be of as high a quality as hardback fiction?

EK: There doesn't have to be any difference. There can be and often is but it's not necessarily so. The hardcovers do not necessarily ensure quality. I've read a aweful lot of junky hardbacks. It will tend to have more prestige coming out in hardcover but it doesn't necessarily have more quality. Paperbacks of course sell more copies than hardbacks. If a hardcover book sells 10,000 copies it's considered successful to have made its investment back. In fact 5,000 or 6,000 copies has always been considered break even for hardcover; paperbacks probably 50,000 to 75,000 would be closer to a break even point.

PQ: Which paperback that you've written do you like best?

EK: It's hard to say. I've got 3 children and I would hate to have to tell you which one was my favorite. I've got 17 paperback books. I have several favorites for different reasons. Manhunters, I always liked because I was able to handle something about racial problems, racial discrimination from both sides; which I probably couldn't have done in my earlier days in paperback but things began to liberalize---Achie Bunker helped. Horsehead Crossing was kind of a personal favorite because I liked the characters and I used a setting that was very familar to me. Buffalo Wagons has always been special to me because for one thing it won me my first Spur Award. Another thing, I got engrossed in research about buffalo hunters. I was pretty well satisfied when I finished that book. For the ability I had at that time, I think I did the best I could possibly have done. I was very well satisfied with it when I turned it loose.

27

I can't say thats always been the case.

PQ: You have won three Spur Awards. Does that imediately increase the sale of your books?

EK: *It certainly helped. I don't know if it has helped so much with the public but it sure has opened the door to the publishing field.*

PQ: Do you think the public is very aware of the Spur Award?

EK: *Not much. I can't see that they can tell. Ace must think it's worth something because they have made a point to try to buy the reprint rights to all the Spur Award books they possibly can. When they [Ace] come out with Buffalo Wagons [probably within the next year] they will have all three of my Spur Awards.*

PQ: Are western writers discriminated against as far as payment for originals (that is, do other types-- detective, adventure, science fiction, etc--bring in more money)?

EK: *For the unit sales they probably are by enlarge... a pretty even breakdown. On a unit basis, most books,whatever the category,your payscale is based on a percentage of retail price. If you sale "X" number of copies, your going to draw so many cents per copy.*

PQ: Do westerns sell better in particular areas of the U.S.? Which areas?

EK: *Oh yes, they sell better west of the Mississippi River and in the South.*

PQ: Your book, The Time It Never Rained, is about the drought of the 1950's. Your newest book, The Good Old Boys, centers around a wet year.

EK: I've used rain in my new book, The Good Old Boys, because, for plot purposes, I needed it to be a good year. I asked my dad about it and he said, "Well, there's 1906, there's 1919, there's 1941, and 1957." In 70 some odd years he had seen 4 good wet years. So I picked 1906, it fitted my story.

PQ: Does material for your books come from personal experiences?

EK: To some extent my dad was part of my character in The Time It Never Rained. I took quite a bit of stuff from my dad, grandad, and my grandmother. I didn't lift anybody 100% of true life except one character. I borrow from a lot of family stories and old stories that I heard when I was a kid, some I heard in recent times. I use a lot of that in my stories, maybe I will change them to fit my type of character or plot needs but they will be grounded in something real.

PQ: Does Doubleday ever solicit books from you?

EK: A new one I'm working on was solicited by them. They asked me last summer at the Western Writers Convention if I could do a book on a particular subject. I hadn't even thought about it; it hit me cold and I said,"I'm sure I can." And, so I am; but its turning into a big job. It is kind of a massive research program. I'm 200 pages into it. I'm writing about black cavalry in Fort Concho during frontier days. I'm paralleling a black soldier with a Comanche Indian; telling both their stories but the black soldier will probably be two thirds of the book and the Indian one third. Then at the very end of the book, their lives come together. Historically, during what you consider the Comanche Indian fighting years after the Civil War, the soldiers who were on the front lines were mostly black. It started out that they put black forces in Texas and other southern states more or less as a [front] against the white people.

29

Gradually this sort of phased out but the black
soldiers were already here and they used them
against the Indians.

Y720 **BB** AN ORIGINAL BALLANTINE WESTERN 40¢

A THUNDERING NOVEL
OF THE RANGE WAR
BY

ELMER KELTON

SPUR AWARD WINNER
FOR BEST WESTERN

BARBED WIRE

COLLECTING ARMED SERVICES EDITIONS
------Charlotte Laughlin

Current nostalgia, coupled with a growing interest in popular culture, often transforms the humble objects of past decades into today's highly sought collectors' items. Such is the case with the Armed Services Editions, which were issued in paperback during World War II for American enlisted men.

When I first became interested in collecting Armed Services Editions, I asked my father, a veteran of World War II, if he remembered having read any. He could not recall having heard of them; but when I showed him a few samples, he remembered having read some of them while he was stationed in the Philippines. I asked if he still had any Armed Services Editions among his books; and he answered, "Oh, no. We just read them and passed them on. They weren't the sort of books anyone would want to keep."

This attitude, shared by millions of American soldiers, is one of the reasons that Armed Services Editions are fairly rare today. Plans for the ASE as a project of the Council on Books in Wartime were announced in *"Publishers' Weekly* of May 22, 1944, with the frequently repeated assertion, "Armed Services Editions will be strictly expendable. They will be distributed to military and naval units in packages containing copies of each title published in a given month, with the idea that service men can then exchange the different titles among themselves."1

When Colonel C. L. Frederick, of the Armed Air Forces, reported to the Council of Books in Wartime in February of 1944, he elaborated on the short life span of the average ASE book. "Fortunately [ASE] books are well made. In the Pacific, insects, vermin, and tropical conditions disintegrate books."2
Colonel Frederick also cited a survey which showed that books ranked above athletics in popularity and use for the soldiers' leisure time. This popularity also took a toll on the survival of the typical ASE book.

On February 1, 1945, Lieutenant Colonel Ray L. Trautman spoke to the third annual meeting of the Council on Books in Wartime and described the reception of ASE books.

> One thing which impressed me is the short life these books have under combat conditions. One or two readings is all that can be counted on. A man reads a book to death very quickly while standing in the rain or snow without any shelter to keep the pages dry.
> It is not unusual for a man to tear off the portion of a book he has finished to give it to the next man who doesn't have a book to read saying--'I'll save my pages for you.'[3]

In short, the ASE books were not intended to last very long, and the conditions under which they were read assured that they would not. Another factor which contributes to the difficulty of collecting ASE books today is the manner in which they were originally distributed. From September of 1943 through June of 1944, one series of thirty titles, in a minimum printing of 50,000 each, was released each month. Each series was given a letter of the alphabet. The first nine series, A-I were alike in distribution as well as number. At the overseas Supply Division of the New York Port of Embarkation, the books of each series were assembled into sets of thirty, weighing 7½ pounds and consisting of one copy of each title. Beginning with the J series, the number in each series was increased to 32 titles and later to 40 titles beginning with the Q series. (Eventually the letter prefixes were discontinued). From New York they were mailed overseas by the Army Postal Service.[4]
But the early announcements in *Publishers' Weekly* make it clear that even from the beginning of the project some of the ASE books were sent to military hospitals and "posts in this country without library facilities."[5]

Nevertheless, the *Library Journal* is correct in
asserting that distribution practices were changed with
series I, in August of 1944. Starting then, a larger
percentage of ASE books were distributed in this country
(The exact percentage I have not yet been able to
ascertain. Can any ASE collector help me on this question?) The *Library Journal* states that beginning with
series I, ASE books were to be distributed to general
hospitals within the United States; and it adds that
in addition to general hospitals, station hospitals in
the United States were also to be added to the distribution list. [6]

Since more copies of the later series were distributed within the United States and since by the end
of the second year the 50,000 copies per title had been
raised to as high as 155,000 copies per title, scattered
examples of these are reasonably easy for the collector
to find. The earlier editions, however, which were
issued primarily to enlisted men serving overseas, are
much harder to come by. A complete set is indeed a
rarity. The Amelia Gayle Gorgas Library of the University of Alabama boasts such a set. PQ has written them
twice concerning availability and origination of this
collection but have had no response.

The cultural importance of this program was carefully examined during the war years by *Publisher's
Weekly, The Saturday Review of Literature,* and even
The Saturday Evening Post. Publishers and booksellers
alike were aware that the carefully selected Armed
Services Editions were both shaping and reflecting the
reading tastes of a large section fo the American public.
Of the first 774 titles issued, fiction made up 60%.
Historical novels with 11%, mysteries with 6%, contemp-
ory fiction with 16%, and humorus books with 12%
were in line with current trends and forcasts. What
surprised everyone about the reading habits of the
soldiers was the unusually high percentage of westerns
(10%) and short stories (6%).[7]

ASE books were designed for the soldier in mind.
The pocket-size ASE were printed in a horizontal format
with two space-saving columns. The horizontal format
was designed to be the most economical printing method.

ASE books were printed on idle presses which normally printed magazines but since the magazine size was to large and bulky, the ASE books were printed in pairs.[8] The upper half of a page was one book and the lower half another. After printed and perhaps even after binding, the two books were "axed" into.[9]

ASE books were printed in two standard sizes, shorter books (less than 320 words) measured 5½ X 3 & 7/8th inches and the longer books (up to 512 words) measured 6½ X 4½ inches. The type for the small book was set 13½ picas wide and having two columns per page running 20 picas deep with a pica space between columns. For the large books, the type was set 15½ picas wide running 22½ picas deep. The type used to print the books ranged from 7½ to 11 point type.[10]

Most books were complete and unabridged except for a few that were condensed because of the 512 page limit. On the bottom front cover of most ASE books it is stated: "This Is A Complete Book--Not A Digest." The few books that were condensed (for example #N31 Charles Dickens' David Copperfield) indicates that it is "Condensed For Wartime Reading." A great deal of "unessential" material such as check lists, appendices, illustrations, indexes, etc were not included from the original publication in order to save space.[11] Often times, dedications, forwords, or other material considered to be essential was printed in italic and either at the end or beginning of the book.

The ASE covers were "printed by offset lithography or letterpress in four flat colors, red, yellow, blue, and black. Each cover carries a half tone photograph in black of the original jacket." [12]

The ASE books were printed on Webb presses using curved nickle-faced stereo types or electrotype. As of September 1943, three printing plants were being used: Street & Smith(who at that time were the publishers of the well known *Astounding* pulp magazine, the format of which, not surprisingly, was approximately twice the size of the small ASE books), the Rumford Press, and Western Printing and Lithographing Co. As many as eight other plants were helping with the composition work. To bind the books together, a combination of waterproof glue and rust resistant staples were employed.[13]

Distribution for overseas was determined on the basis of the number of soldiers: one set per month for each 150 men or fraction thereof and one set per month for each 50 hospital beds. For distribution to American Prisoners of War, four thousand sets per month were sent to the War Prisoners' Aid of the Y.M.C.A. First priority was given to hospitalized soldiers and to soldiers in fighting zones or isolated outposts.[14]

Armed Services Editions, Inc. was a non-profit corporation under the direction of Philip Van Doren Stern which sold books to the Army and Navey at cost; the royality being fixed at one cent per copy to be devided between the original publisher and author.[15] The cost to the taxpayer not counting distribution costs was estimated to be only 6¢ per book.

An appointed upaid Advisory Committee consisting of publishers, librarians, booksellers, editors, and critics was established to select which books would be printed as ASE books. Once a book was approved by this Advisory Committee, a recommendation was forwarded to the Special Services Division and to the Navy Department for agreement. Book selections which passed this triple review were subjected to the book reviewing section of the Armed Services Editions, Inc. Only after passing this fourfold screening process were arrangements made for printing ASE books. [16]

From the first, it was stressed that selections for ASE books would exclude any controversial or specialized books. The Army turned down Professors Franz Boas' Mind of Primitive Man as too "specialized and highbrow"; Dr. Will Durant's The Story of Philosphy as to dated, Letters of Alexander Woollcott as too "coy"; and Some of My Best Friends Are Soldiers because "the title was confusing." [17]

Some of the books were actually banned because of Senator Taft's amendment (the so-called soldiers' vote bill). According to the Saturday Review of Literature, this amendment imposed drastic penalties on any military officers helping anything containing "political argument of political propaganda of any kind designed or

calculated to affect the result of any (Fedral) election"
to reach men in the armed forces. The Army took a
literal interpretation of this amendment and obeyed
it to such an extreme that is some quarters there was
suspicion that the Army deliberately set out to force
repeal of the amendment by carrying it to the ultimate
limit. The Army withdrew 15 books, including Beard's
The Republic and Basic History of the United States;
Summer Welles' The Time for Decision; E.B. White's
Essays, several standard textbooks on American history;
and even AAF, the Official Guide to the Army Air Forces
issued by the Army itself. The AAF was withdrawn because
it contained a portrait of President Roosevelt.[18]

From the Fall of 1943 to October of 1947, an
estimated 1312 titles were printed (123,250,000 copies).
Does any ASE collector have an exact figure?

During the War, ASE books reached a peak of
155,000 copies printed per title per month. From
October 1946 to October 1947, only 25,000 copies per
title per month were printed as the War wound down;
and these were printed in a new shape and size similar
to Pocket Books. This size was more economical for
the smaller printing (25,000 per title).

Some examples of the Armed Services Editions
include:

S6	Frank Gruber	*Peace Marshall*
S20	William Irish	*After-Dinner Story*
S28	Thorne Smith	*The Night Life of the Gods*
R25	Christopher Morley	*Kitty Foyle*
N6	Carl Sandburg	*Selected Poems*
N29	Stuart Cloete	*The Turning Wheels*
Q2	James M. Cain	*The Postman Always Rings Twic*
Q10	A.A. Fair	*Give 'Em the Ax*
S21	Erle Stanley Gardner	*The Case of the Black-Eyed Blonde*
021	Georges Simenon	*On the Danger Line*
022	Edgar Rice Burroughs	*The Return of Tarzan*
P6	Rex Stout	*Not Quite Dead Enough*
906	" "	*" " "*
909	Mary Shelley	*Frankenstein*
745	H.G. Wells	*The War of the Worlds*
751	Raymond Chandler	*The Big Sleep*

791	Ernest Haycox	*Trail Smoke*
747	F & R Lockridge	*Death on the Aisle*
T13	Robert Benchley	*Benchley Beside Himself*
680	Ellery Queen	*Calamity Town*
966	James Hilton	*So Well Remembered*
J285	James Gould Cozzens	*The Last Adam*
012	C S Forester	*The African Queen*
1021	W C Tuttle	*The Wolf Pack of Lobo Butte*
663	Brett Halliday	*Murder and the Married Virgin*

Notes:

[1]Publisher's Weekly, vol 143: 1966-7, May 22, 1943.

[2]Publisher's Weekly, vol 145: 719, Feb. 10, 1944.

[3]"Council on Books Holds Third Annual Meeting," Publisher's Weekly, vol 147: 741, Feb. 10, 1945.

[4]"What Our Soldiers Are Reading," Library Journal, vol 70: 148-9, Feb. 15, 1945.

[5]"Currents in the Trade," Publisher's Weekly, vol 144: 901, Sept. 11, 1943.

[6]Op. Cit., "What Our Soldiers Are Reading,"LJ v70.

[7]"What the Armed Forces Read," Publisher's Weekly, vol 148: 1647, Oct 6, 1945.

[8]Op. Cit.,"Currents in the Trade," PW vol 144.

[9]Saturday Review of Literature, vol 28: 18, Aug. 11, 1945.

[10]Op. Cit.,"Currents in the Trade,"PW vol 144.

[11]Ibid.

[12]Ibid.

[13]Ibid.

[14]Op. Cit.,"What Our Soldiers Are Reading,"LJ,v 70.

[15]Op. Cit., SRL, vol 28: 18 Aug 11, 1945.

[16]Op. Cit.,"What Our Soldiers Are Reading,"LJ,v 70.

[17]"Censoritis, War & Navy Departments Ruling on Several Distinguished Books," Saturday Review of Literature, vol 27: 12, July 1, 1944.

[18]Ibid.

THE MYSTERIOUS STRANGER

A FANTASY BY

MARK TWAIN

Overseas edition for the Armed Forces. Distributed by the Special Services Division, A.S.F. for the Army, and by the Bureau of Naval Personnel for the Navy. U. S. Government property. Not for sale. Published by Editions for the Armed Services, Inc., a non-profit organization established by the Council on Books in Wartime.

THIS IS THE COMPLETE BOOK—NOT A DIGEST

Barefoot Boy With Cheek

BY

MAX SHULMAN

MAX SHULMAN

Overseas edition for the Armed Forces. Distributed by the Special Services Division, A.S.F. for the Army, and by the Bureau of Naval Personnel for the Navy. U. S. Government property. Not for sale. Published by Editions for the Armed Services, Inc., a non-profit organization established by the Council on Books in Wartime.

THIS IS THE COMPLETE BOOK—NOT A DIGEST

THE GREEN DOOR MYSTERY
------Howard Waterhouse

In 1963 Pyramid Books began a series of reprint mystery classics which has become a good series to collect. Green Door Mysteries are collectable because they are relatively recent (can still be found in secondhand shops and yard sales), because the series is relatively short (finding 50 to 60 items will encompass the core of the series), and because they contain some of the best works of the authors who are represented.

A look at the check list will show that the editor(s) had obvious preferences since Rex Stout and Anthony Gilbert are proportionally over represented. However, that editorial bias was advantageous for the present day reader as the series provides access to books that in first editions would be almost all prohibitively priced. That is to say that these editors picked books that would still be winners in the future, whereas so many series of the past now seem filled with authors we don't really want to read. The concept and scope of the series is evident in the first few items where the aim seems to be to provide quality books with an overall unity. The covers at the outset had an attractive design with a green spine which wrapped over onto the front cover and appeared as a door frame, with the door opening inward on the title and a small illustration. Hanging on the door (a nice touch) we find a small green skull as a knocker. This design format was continued up to number 961 when the green spine and door frame disappeared, while the door itself was retained. The problem for the collector at this point is that the books are less readily identifiable when seen on the shelf. Although the words "Green Door Mystery" and familiar pyramid remain, one has to look more closely.

Another bit of evidence pointing to a good original concept which became watered down, was the inclusion of author biographical sketches in the first few books. (Such paragraphs ended with number 932 as far as I can find.) These biographies were printed on the back of the half title and were essentially thumbnail sketches, a touch of class which later came to be replaced by ads for other books in the series.

Starting with book number 960 the spines are white with varied colored pyramids except for 961 and 1067 (old fashioned green) and number 1269 which has a black spine and symbolizes the end of the over all "Green Door" concept.   These do not contain the door at all except in a small logo up in the corner of the front cover which was to appear on the few remaining books which are called "Green Door" but are evidently only hang-overs from the originally well planned and unified approach.

In presenting the following check list, I'm indebted to Rich Butler of Brooklyn, New York who did some of the preliminary research.

R 822	Rex Stout	*Not Quite Dead Enough*
		Feb 63
R 823	Mabel Seeley	*The Crying Sisters*
		Feb 63
R 824	F. & R. Lockridge	*The Long Skeleton*
		Feb 63
R 825	Georges Simenon	*Madame Maigret's Own Case*
		Feb 63
R 847	Manning Coles	*Night Train To Paris*
		April 63
R 872	J.J. Marric	*Gideon's Night*
		June 63
R 873	J.P. Marquand	*Ming Yellow*
		June 63
R 884	F. & R. Lockridge	*Voyage Into Violence*
		July 63
R 894	Rex Stout	*Too Many Cooks*
		Aug 63
R 895	Patricia Wentworth	*The Fingerprint*
		Aug 63
R 906	Anthony Gilbert	*Dark Death*
		Aug 63
R 917	Rex Stout	*Black Orchids*
		Sept 63

R 919	Rex Stout	League Of Frightened Men Oct 63
R 920	Phoebe Atwood Taylor	Proof Of The Pudding Oct 63
R 931	Rex Stout	Some Buried Caesar Nov 63
R 932	Patricia Wentworth	Death At The Deep End Nov 63
R 947	J.J. Marric	Gideon's Week Dec 63
R 960	Rex Stout	Over My Dead Body Jan 64
R 961	Margaret Carpenter	Experiment Perilous Jan 64
R 969	Phoebe Atwood Taylor	Octagon House Feb 64
R 970	Rex Stout	Fer-De-Lance Feb 64
R 983	Rex Stout	The Red Box Mar 64
R 984	Anthony Gilbert	A Case For Mr. Crook Mar 64
R 995	Stuart Palmer	The Green Ace Apr 64
R 996	F. & R. Lockridge	First Come, First Kill Apr 64
R 1008	Nicholas Blake	Malice With Murder May 64
R 1009	Mabel Seeley	The Listening House May 64
R 1025	Rex Stout	Double For Death Jun 64
R 1026	Joel Townslet Rogers	The Red Right Hand Jun 64
R 1040	Stuart Palmer	Cold Poison Jul 64
R 1041	Anthony Gilbert	After The Verdict Jul 64
R 1053	Rex Stout	The Rubber Band Aug 64
R 1054	Mabel Seeley	The Whistling Shadow Aug 64

R 1066 Rex Stout   *The Hand In The Glove*
                          Sep 64
R 1067 Ira Levin   *A Kiss Before Dying*
                          Sep 64
R 1082 Maurice Proctor   *Somewhere In This City*
                          Oct 64
R 1083 John Dickson Carr *The Men Who Explained
                          Miracles*   Oct 64
R 1098 Rex Stout   *Red Threads*
                          Nov 64
R 1099 Dorothy B. Hughes *The Davidian Report*
                          Nov 64
R 1107 Anthony Gilbert   *And Death Came, Too*
                          Dec 64
R 1108 Patricia Wentworth *Poison In The Pen*
                          Dec 64
R 1123 Rex Stout   *The Sound Of Murder*
                          Jan 65
R 1124 Phoebe Atwood Taylor *The Cape Cod Mystery*
                          Jan 65
R 1137 Patricia Wentworth *The Ivory Dagger*
                          Feb 65
R 1138 Maurice Proctor   *The Pub Crawler*
                          Feb 65
R 1149 Rex Stout   *The Broken Vase*
                          Mar 65
R 1150 Anthony Gilbert   *Murder Comes Home*
                          Mar 65
R 1166 Rex Stout   *Bad For Business*
                          Apr 65
R 1191 Maurice Proctor   *The Devil Was Handsome*
                          Jun 65
R 1207 Dorothy B. Hughes *The So Blue Marble*
                          Aug 65
R 1231 Patricia Wentworth *The Silent Pool*
                          Sep 65
R 1244 F. & R. Lockridge *Murder Within Murder*
                          Oct 65
R 1258 Anthony Gilbert   *A Question Of Murder*
                          Nov 65 (last one with door)
R 1269 Anthony Gilbert   *Out For The Kill*
                          Dec 65

R 1282	Philip MacDonald	*Guest In The House* Jan 66
R 1292	Anthony Gilbert	*Death Casts A Long Shadow* 1966
R 1542	Anthony Boucher	*The Case Of The Seven Sneezes* Dec 66
R 1585	Anthony Boucher	*The Case Of The Crumpled Knave* Mar 67
X 1681	Anthony Boucher	*Rocket To The Morgue* Oct 67
X 1682	Patricia Wentworth	*The Summerhouse* Aug 67
X 1733	Anthony Boucher	*The Case Of The Solid Gold Key* Jan 68

So far as this writer knows that brings the series up through 1968 where, it seems, commercial interest and current vogue combined to finish off this little series devoted to golden crime puzzles behind the Green Door.

CHECK LISTS
FOR SALE:

Each Check List Gives Publisher, Number, Author, Title, and Date. (Postpaid)

ACE: D1-D411 1952-59 (11 pages).......$2.50

AVON: 1-864 1941-59 (16 pages)........:..$3.50

DELL: 1-1590 1942-59 (19 pages)........$3.50

POPULAR LIBRARY:1-787 1943-59(16 pages).$3.50

Armed Services Editions: 1-1322
          1943-47 (40 pages).........$5.00

BUNKER BOOKS P.O. BOX 1638, SPRING VALLEY, CAL.
          92077

PYRAMID BOOKS R-625 50¢

Inspector Maigret calls on his wife in
the case the police couldn't solve

georges
SIMENON

Madame Maigret's
Own Case

"A fascinating story . . ."—St. Louis Post-Dispatch

A PQ Interview With:

JADA DAVIS

PQ: According to <u>Cumulative Paperback Index</u>, you have written two paperbacks, <u>One For Hell</u> (1953, Red Seal #24) and <u>The Outraged Sect</u> (1956, Avon #713). Have you written others? Do you plan to publish any in the future? Why after two novels did you quit writing?

JD: *I didn't quit writing, although I've done little the past two years. I've written fifteen novels, but have only five I really like. My agent, Ingrid Hallen, retired years ago. I've had only one since--and he lost a novel I'd spent two years researching and writing. I hope to retire early and resume the career I should never have abandoned.*

PQ: Why did you start writing? How did you break into the market? Did you first have an agent?

JD: *I sold my first story at fifteen--a short to Liberty magazine. I can't remember when I started writing, but I can't remember when I didn't have the desire. I submitted my first novel when I was eighteen---to Random House, I think. It was returned with a letter that told me I had raw talent--but that I had tried too hard to write like Thomas Wolfe. I don't like to admit it, but I'd never heard of Thomas Wolfe. After reading him, I threw my novel into a trash barrel behind the Odessa American (where I was sports editor).*
I submitted a second novel while attending the University of Texas and received what I believed was a letter of rejection. My creative writing professor saw the letter a year later and almost had apoplexy. He pointed out that the editor only asked for some re-writing. I still have

that novel in its original form.

I accepted a job with Southwestern Bell a few years later and showed a manuscript to a friend. He told Margaret Lucas, a scout for Random House, and she asked to see it. Random House suggested I get some paperbacks published but insisted on first look and opportunity. In my mind, that was unfair. (Oh, to be able to turn back the pages). Jessyca Russell was publishing Writer's Newsletter in New York. Lucas told her about me and she sold One For Hell a week later. Meanwhile, she arranged for Ingrid Hallen to represent me. Fawcett wanted me to sign a long-term contract, and Hallen rejected that on my behalf. (Oh, to be able to turn back the pages).

PQ: Why did you choose Avon and Red Seal to publish your books? Did either of your books every come out in hardback?

JD: Jessyca Russell chose Fawcett [Red Seal] and Hallen chose Avon.

PQ: What writer or book influenced your writing the most? Why?

JD: Wolfe was an influence--when I finally read him-- but only, I think, because he excited my desire to write. I found Hemingway contrived...yet, I think all authors influenced me...because each had something to offer. If I had to pin one down, I'd name Dickens. Why--because I'd read nothing but battered copies of True Detective and Wild West Weekly until an old man (a neighbor) opened a musty trunk and gave me an arm load of even mustier books. They were treasures. I still had my battered copy of Oliver Twist when, years later, I went into the army.

PQ: Which of your books do you like best? Why?

JD: *I have at least two novels better than One For Hell or The Outraged Sect (in my opinion). In fact, I think I'll drag them out and dust them off. Of the published two, I think I prefer One For Hell. Both were based on actual events (Fawcett sent a man to Odessa [Texas] to find out why the tremendous sale of a paperback. Grocers had them stacked on counters with signs that said, "Read about people you know." It scared Fawcett out of their skulls. Actually, the characters were composites--and the events disguised.*

Answers to Quiz on page 13:

a. 4.   h. 1.
b. 7.   i. 8.
c. 9.   j. 3.
d. 2.   k. 6.
e. 12.   l. 14.
f. 5.   m. 10.
g. 11.   n. 13.

ALMURIC
Or "Edgar Rice Burroughs
Visits the Hyborian Age"
------Michael T. Smith

Ask a modern heroic-fantasy writer what two writers
influenced him most, and nine times out of ten the
answer will be Robert E. Howard and Edgar Rice Burroughs.
Howard, by solidifying the elements of sword-and-sorcery
fantasy, and Burroughs, by pioneering the scientific
romance stories of swords and ray guns on exotic planets,
have affected writers as well as readers of fantastic
fiction throughout this century.

Almuric, Howard's single sword-and-planet novel,
recently printed in its first widely distributed paperback edition by Berkley Medallion, with a full color
cover and a matching pull-out poster by Ken Kelley,
is an interesting blend of the two approaches.

Many of the standard Burroughs devices are present.
There is the first person narrative by an Earthman
(Esau Cairn), transported by mystical or pseudo-scien-
tific means to an exotic planet. There is the presence
on this planet (Almuric) of a human race (the Guras)
and an inhuman one (the Yagas). There are the periods
of captivity which Cairn endures on Almuric (a favorite
Burroughs device). And Cairn's eventual mating with
a "princes"--of sorts--of the Guras recalls both the
Mars and Venus stories of E.R.B.

Nor can the similarity of Howard's Guras, with
their beautiful women and ape-like men, to Burroughs
Aparians be over-looked. And the episodes of Cairn
surviving in the wilderness remind the reader of
Burroughs' The Cave Girl, among others.

Yet, from the very first page, it is evident
that Howard, not Burroughs, is the spinner of this
yarn. Esau Cairn, like most of R.E.H.'s modern
heroes, was born and reared in the Southwest. Unlike
Burroughs' gentlemanly warriors, he is a throwback to
an earlier, more primitive type of man--an inherent
savage whose barbaric temperament and preternatural
strength has made him a fugitive from justice. And,
rather than a swordsman, he has been a professional

boxer in the tradition of Steve Costigan and Dennis
Dogan--a far cry from "Virginia gentleman" John Carter!
Cairn is a "man out of his time"--the same kind of man
Howard fancied himself to be.

Unfortunately, many of Howard's faults are also
all too evident. For one thing, his inhuman race, the
Yagas are almost identical to the winged man from "The
Garden of Fear." Also, the Guras religion is basically
that of the Cimmerians' Crom. Even the name of their
deity, Thak, is familiar from the Conan story "Rogues
in the House." And the names of some of the Guras
themselves, such as Ghor and Bragi, can be recognized
from a score of stories.

Howard's overuse of one sound in a phrase is also
prominent--the Yagas live "in the grim city of Yugga,
on the rock Yuthla, by the river Yogh, in the land of
Yagg..." (It must be noted that "Yaga" and "Yagg"
sound suspiciously similar to "Yag-Kosha"
from"The Tower of the Elephant"). And Howard again
indulges in his deplorable habit of avoiding a des-
cription of something by calling it "indescribable" or
"too horrible for words."

Of one fight scene, Howard says, "There is little
to be said of that fight," then goes on to spend a page
and a half describing it. Later, he says, "As this is
a chronicle and not an essay, I can scarcely skim the
surface of customs, ways, and traditions"--this, in the
midst of a nine page "essay"!

Almuric is, essentially, a transplanted Hyborian
Age, with warring city-states, ancient ruined cities,
and fearsome monsters aplenty. The Howard story which
Almuric most resembles is "Beyond the Black River"--
not in plot, but in theme and subject matter. Both
tales are paeons of praise of barbarism. Indeed,
concerning the Guras, Howard states that they reached
the level of barbarism, then "seemingly defying laws
wer on Earth have come to regard as immutable, they
remain stationary, neither advancing nor retogressing"-
Howard's idea of the perfect society.

The tale does have its strong points though.
Esau Cairn is a fascinating character. The battle
scenes, as always, are exciting. Howard's knack for

portraying a sense of the rise and fall of civilizations stands him in good stead. And if the Guras and Yagas aren't necessarily very original, Howard's other creatures, notably the dog-headed demons and the Blind Ones, are.

And even if you don't like the story, Ken Kelley's beautiful poster alone is worth half the price.

The question comes to mind of whether R.E.H. ever intended to write a sequel to <u>Almuric</u>. The story apparently didn't cause much enthusiasm when it first appeared in *Weird Tales*, else it would have been reprinted before now. Yet the ending leaves many things unexplained and many mysteries unexplored. One could almost wish the book had been reprinted by Zebra rather than Berkley, so that we could possibly look forward to more chapters in this, one of the most interesting peices of Howardiana.

NOTICE:

The 1978 World Fantasy Convention will be held in Fort Worth, Texas on October 13, 14, and 15, 1978. Michael Templin, 1309 S. West, Arlington, Texas 76010 is the 1978 Chairman. The Convention will honor the late Robert E. Howard.

Make plans now to attend.

ROBERT E. HOWARD'S LIBRARY
A Checklist

As promised in volume 1 number 1 of Paperback Quarterly, this issue and the next two issues will provide a checklist of the books found on the accession list at Howard Payne University and believed to have been in the Robert E. Howard Memorial Collection. It's not surprising that 11 of the following 66 books (16%) are written by Edgar Rice Burroughs.

Abdullah and Pakinham.	*Dreamers of Empire*
Adam, G. Mercer.	*The Life Of David Crockett*
Aesop's Fables	
Aiken, Conrad	*American Poetry 1671-1928*
Aison, Greta.	*Modern American Poetry*
Alger, Horatio.	*A Young Miner*
Alger, Horatio.	*Tom The Bootblack*
Alger, Horatio	*The Tin Box*
Alger, Horatio	*Joes Luck*
Alger, Horatio.	*Mark Masons Truimph*
Alger, Horatio.	*The Cash Boy*
Alger, Horatio.	*Only An Irish Boy*
Allen, E.A.	*The Prehistoric World*
Ansley, Henry.	*I Like The Depression*
Arlitt, Ada Hart.	*Adolescence Psychology*
Bansittart, Robert.	*Singing Caravan*
Beach, R.	*Son Of Gods*
Benet, Stephen	*John Browns Body*
Bower, B.M.	*Chip Of The Flying U*
Branom, Mendel E.	*Teaching Of Geography*
Bunyan, John	*The Holy War*
Burns, Walter Noble	*Tombstone*
Burroughs, Edgar R.	*At The Earths Core*
Burroughs, Edgar R.	*Tarzan The Terrible*
Burroughs, Edgar R.	*Tarzan Of The Apes*
Burroughs, Edgar R.	*Son Of Tarzan*
Burroughs, Edgar R.	*Tarzan And Jewels Of Opar*
Burroughs, Edgar R.	*Return Of Tarzan*
Burroughs, Edgar R.	*Princess Of Mars*
Burroughs, Edgar R.	*The Musker*

Burroughs, Edgar R.	Warland Of Mars
Burroughs, Edgar R.	Gods Of Mars
Burroughs, Edgar R.	Thuvia, Maid Of Mars
Call, Clement	Guns Of The Gods
Caret, Theodore	Adventures Of An African Slaver
Castro, Adolphe	Portrait Of Ambiose Bierce
Chambers, Robert W.	America Or The Sacrifice
Chambers, Robert W.	The Drums Of Aulone
Chambers, Robert W.	The Maid AT Arms
Chambers, Robert W.	Slayer Of Souls
Chambers, Robert W.	The Little Red Foot
Chapman	What Bird Is That
	Comptons Pictured Encyclopedia
Comstock	Hanbook Of Nature Study
Cooper	A History Of The Rod
Cooper, James	A Tale
Corbett, James	Roar Of The Crowd
Crane, Wathalia	Laua Lane
Cunningham	Trigonometry
Curwood, James O.	Valley Of Silent Men
Darratt and Long	English Poems
Dickens, Charles	Nicholas Nickleby
Digby, Bassett	Tigers Gold And Witch Doctors
Dixon	Life Of Billy Dixon
Dobie, J. Frank	Doronado's Children
Downey	The Grand Turke
Doyle, A. Conan	The Sign Of The Four
Doyle, A. Conan	The Maracot Deep
Doyle, A. Conan	Hound Of The Baskervilles
Doyle, A. Conan	His Last Bow
Doyle, A. Conan	Conan Doyle's Best Books
Doyle, A. Conan	The Firm of Girdlestone
Doyle, A. Conan	The Lost World
Doyle, A. Conan	Return Of Sherlock Holmes
Draper	Curriculum Making
Duval, John	Adventures Of Big Foot Wallace

The Outraged Sect
by Jada Davis
(Avon, 1956) 143 pp. $0.25

Jada Davis published only two paperback originals
in the 1950s, of which this was the second. (The other
was One For Hell, Fawcett Red Seal Book #24). Set in
the closing days of WW II, The Outraged Sect tells the
story of Book Morris, returned war hero, now a newspaperman, and his efforts to prevent mob action against
the Sect (probably modeled on the Jehovah's Witnesses).
The citizens of Book's hometown are stirred to action
by the corrupt sheriff who, like most of the others in
the town, can't understand the Sect's refusal to salute
the flag, fight, or participate in the war. Violence
naturally breakes out. Members of the Sect are beaten,
and one is killed. Morris himself is beaten several
times, but not as often as he beats the villains.
The novel has an irresistible narrative drive,
partly because the reader just knows that the bad guys
have to get it in the end (they do) and partly because
Davis is a mile-a-minute storyteller. The marvel is
that in such a context this story was told at all:
its sensibility is much more that of the 1960s than
that of the supposedly head-in-sand Eisenhower years.
Morris's defense of the Sect's pacificism is so well-
informed and on-target that if this book had been issued in hardcover, someone would probably have "dis-
covered" it during the Vietnam caper and revived it.
The evil sheriff even tries to manage (or suppress)
the news.
The book's major flaw is the fact that the bad
guys are all really bad and Book Morris is really good,
but this effect is softened by the appearance of characters who want to side with Book but don't, for various reasons. Their hearts are pure, but they can't
quite bring themselves to fight for what they believe.
Too, by the novel's end even Book has become exasper-
ated with the Sect's refusal to fight. He carries on

more because he has to than because he wants to.

I'd like to know how many "serious" novels of 1956 raised the same issues brought up by Jada Davis. And I wonder (melodrama aside) how many dealt with them as thoughtfully and as well.

------Bill Crider

Brothers in Confidence
by David Madden
(Avon, 1972) 173 pp. $0.95

No need to mince words: this is a good book. Everyone who has worked in the area of popular culture for very long has run across the name of David Madden. For one thing, he's the editor of an essential book, Tough Guy Writers of the Thirties. This novel shows that he not only edited the later book, but that he absorbed its lessons. There's not a wasted line or word in Brothers in Confidence.

The novel is the story of three brothers, Traven, Hollis, and Cody Weaver. Traven and Cody are con men (passing hot checks is their game), and Hollis is the member of the family who goes to college and gets a job teaching English. But first, and this is the story, he has to try to keep Cody off the chain gang to which he is about to be sentenced for plying his trade. Hollis tells it all in his own voice, in a narrative informed with the spirit of the movies and the comics of the thirties and forties, but filled at the same time with a love of good writing and storytelling that amounts almost to awe. It's both tough and touching by turns, with no false notes.

There's never been any real doubt in my mind that significant fiction has appeared in paperback original editions. This book simply confirms that notion.

-------Bill Crider

Question and Answer
by Poul Anderson
(Ace Books, 1956, 1978) 147 pp. $1.50
cover art by Michael Whelan

Behind this science fiction novel by Poul Anderson lies a very interesting history. According to the author's preface, a professional scientist designed a suitably earth-like planet and named it Troas. He then gave the author and two other well known science fiction writers, James Blish and Isaac Asimov, the basic information that the first earth expedition to his imaginary planet was never heard of again. Each writer proceeded to finish the story from this, and all three were to be published in a single volume. Such plans did not work out however, and each was published separately. Anderson's version first appeared in *Amazing* and later in paperback under the title Planet Of No Return (Ace Books #D-199, 1956).

In Question and Answer, the earth has finally been populated to its limits, the Moon, Mars, and Jovian moons have also been colonized, but only at a great expense. Scientists have searched for over a generation for a suitable Earth-like planet to colonize, but with no success. Astronomers accidently stumble upon such a planet which they name Troas. An Earth exploratory expedition is sent to investigate colonization possibilities, but is never heard from again. Anderson's book deals with the efforts and adventures of the second Troas expedition, whose ill-assorted crew sets out to answer the question of what happened to the first Troas expedition. What follows is a suspense filled, captivating novel well worth reading.

--------Shawn Loudermilk

6. Some readers may have been interested enough in the Harry Whittington interview in issue #1 to begin collecting his works. Here's some bad new for them. According to Whittington, the listing of his works in *Contemporary Authors* is "about correct" (at least as far as the titles are concerned) "except for 38 novels which I did once a month and none of which appeared under my own or my own pen names." These novels were sent to the author's agent, and Whittington does not even know the titles under which they appeared.

7. Dell Mystery Novels No. 1 (January-March, 1955) featured three short novels: "A Bundle for the Coroner" by Brett Halliday, "But the Prophet Died" by William Campbell Gault, and "The Quiet Woman" by Bruno Fischer. The editors would like to hear from anyone owning subsequent issues in this series. (How many issues were there? What writers were featured?)

8. John Jakes is, as everyone knows by now, the wildly successful author of the paperback original Bicentennial Series for Pyramid (now HBJove). He is also (apparently) the author of Gonzaga's Woman. (We say "apparently" because this book is not included in Jakes' listing in *Contemporary Authors*.) Gonzaga's Woman is advertised in the back of Beacon Book #B-130 as being available by mail order. Its order number is B-115. The editors, however, have a copy of Royal Books Giant Edition #22, a double book containing Talbot Munday's Affair in Araby and Jakes' Gonzaga's Woman. The copyright page for the latter states that it is "a wholly original work, never before published in any form." Can anyone tell us what's going on here?

9. An interesting and puzzling paperback is Pocket Book #116, Erle Stanley Gardner's The Case of the Howling Dog. Pocket Books provide by far the best printing history than any other paperback publisher; a fact that bibliographers are just now beginning to appreciate. But how reliable are these printing

histories? I have two copies of Pocket Book #116 which have different covers because they are different printings. However, they both indicate that they are printing 19. On closer examination, the following printing date inconsistances are revealed:

Book #1			Book #2		
14th printing	..Dec 1944		14th printing	..Dec 1944	
15th	"	..Jan 1945	15th	"	..Jan 1945
16th	"	..Feb 1945	16th	"	..Jun 1945
17th	"	..Mar 1945	17th	"	..Oct 1945
18th	"	..May 1945	18th	"	..Feb 1946
19th	"	..Oct 1945	19th	"	..Nov 1946

Ads at the back of each book reveal that Book #1 is the earlier publication. Is one of the printing histories in error or are both incorrect? What printing histories do other Pocket Book #116 have? [Editor's Note: We have written Pocket Books for an explanation but as of this printing, we have had no response.]

10. I recently picked up a Pocket Book paperback #259 entitled Halfway House by Ellery Queen. I didn't really know what I had, at first, until I examined it more closely. I found that I had an experimental book but what really excited me was a business reply card still intact in the center of the book. The card contained eight short questions concerning reader choices. It is the first time that I have ever seen it, even though it was published and sent out on or before April 1944. The book was produced with the same horizontal format and double columns as the Armed Services Editions. I'm curious, naturally as to how many were printed. Was it distributed the same way as the regular editions? Was it only sent out to a select list of readers, collectors, or book dealers? Was this the only experimental book as such?

                          ------M.C. Hill
                            Spring Valley, CA

HOWARD WATERHOUSE

BOX 167

WEST UPTON, MA.

01587

617 - 529 - 3703

WANTS:

MURDER MYSTERY MONTHLY (AVON) 6,7,9,27,28,
    39,43,46,47,48

DELL MAP BACKS 38,55,89,152

PYRAMID GREEN DOOR 822,1054,1292

He has for SALE or TRADE hundred's of

DELLS, POPULAR LIBRARY, POCKET BOOKS,

BANTAMS, as well as Digest sized mysteries

of the 40's.

PLEASE SEND WANTS OR REQUEST LIST.

BUNKER BOOKS   P.O. BOX 1638 SPRING VALLEY, CA   92077

These were published and distributed from 1940 to 1943.
They all measure 4 &3/8th X 6 inches and are either
blue, black, or green in color, have 100 pages, and
generally have a red rooster head in various sizes somewhere on the front cover. I will pay from $5 to $40
for any, depending on condition and scarcity.
        All titles are not known (1 missing)
        All titles have not been verified (8)
This leaves (20) that have been verified. Any information on any of the unverified will be appreciated and
credit given. I also would like to hear from anybody
who has one or more in their possesion, whether they
want to sell or not. I am in the process of compiling
all known facts and will be submitting for republication
in a national publication.
        The following numbers and titles have been verified.

#	Author	Title
1.	Queen, E.	The Spanish Cape Mystery
3.	Fishbein, M.M.D.	Your health Questions
5.	Currie, S.	How to Make Friends Easily
6.	Gregory, J.	Everybodys Book of Jokes and Wisecracks
7.		Voice of Experience
9.	Engle, W	Enter the G-Men
10.		1000 Facts Worth Knowing
11.	Martin, L	How to Win and Hold a Husband
12.	VanLoon, H.W.	Worlds Great Love Affairs
18.	MacIsaac, F.	Love on the Run
19.	Beach, R.	Tower of Flame
20.		Story of Rabelais and Voltaire
21.	Grant, M.	Shadow and the Voice of Murder
22.	Hutton, B	The Green Death
23.	Burroughs, E.R.	Tarzan and the Forbidden City
24.		Humorous Stories and Anecdotes
25.	Chidsey, D.B.	Nobody Heard the Shot
26.	Christie, A.	The Blue Geranium
27.	Wylie, A.	Danger Mansion
28.	Eberhart, M.G.	Stranger in Flight
14.	Striker, F.	The Lone Ranger

This leaves numbers 2,4,8,13,15,16, and 17 to be coupled with the following known titles:

Carnegie, D.   Little Known Facts About Well Known
               People
Christie, A.   Mystery Of Crime In Cabin 66
Christie, A.   Mystery of the Baghdad Chest
               Everybodys Dream Book
               Necronomicon??(may not exist)
               Favorite Poems, Popular Selections
               From The Worlds Literature

This leaves one title unknown

If you have any information concerning BANTAM LOS ANGELES BOOKS Please contact: Bunker Books, P.O. BOX 1638, Spring Valley, California 92077

***** NEW PUBLICATION *****

If you are a reader or collector of Heroic or

Epic Fantasy, Swords & Sorcery, Horror, or Weird

Fiction and want the most up to date information

available on hardbacks, paperbacks, authors, pub-

lishers, etc. in this genre then the PQ highly

recommends FANTASY NEWSLETTER. Be informed!

Subscribe now to FANTASY NEWSLETTER, published by

Paul Allen, 1015 West 36th St., Loveland, Co. 80537

Only $5 per year (12 issues) Well worth the price.

www.ingramcontent.com/pod-product-compliance
Lightning Source LLC
Chambersburg PA
CBHW021224020426
42331CB00003B/454